# ESSAYS IN THE
# ART OF WRITING

MAVEN BOOKS

# Essays in the ART OF WRITING

ROBERT LOUIS STEVENSON

MAVEN BOOKS

Chennai          Trichy          Tirunelveli          New Delhi

MAVEN BOOKS

An Imprint of **MJP Publishers**

ISBN 978-93-88191-65-4  **MAVEN Books**

All rights reserved  No. 44, Nallathambi Street,
Printed and bound in India  Triplicane, Chennai 600 005

MJP  692  © Publishers, 2019

**Publisher :  C. Janarthanan**

# PUBLISHER'S NOTE

The legacy of a country is in its varied cultural heritage, historical literature, developments in the field of economy and science. The top nations in the world are competing in the field of science, economy and literature. This vast legacy has to be conserved and documented so that it can be bestowed to the future generation. The knowledge of this legacy is slowly getting perished in the present generation due to lack of documentation.

Keeping this in mind, the concern with retrospective acquiring of rare books has been accented recently by the burgeoning reprint industry. MAVEN Books is gratified to retrieve the rare collections with a view to bring back those books that were landmarks in their time.

In this effort, a series of rare books would be republished under the banner, "MAVEN Books". The books in the reprint series have been carefully selected for their contemporary usefulness as well as their historical importance within the intellectual. We reconstruct the book with slight enhancements made for better presentation, without affecting the contents of the original edition.

Most of the works selected for republishing covers a huge range of subjects, from history to anthropology. We believe this reprint edition will be a service to the numerous researchers and practitioners active in this fascinating field. We allow readers to experience the wonder of peering into a scholarly work of the highest order and seminal significance.

MAVEN Books

# CONTENTS

# ON SOME TECHNICAL ELEMENTS
# OF STYLE IN LITERATURE

There is nothing more disenchanting to man than to be shown the springs and mechanism of any art. All our arts and occupations lie wholly on the surface; it is on the surface that we perceive their beauty, fitness, and significance; and to pry below is to be appalled by their emptiness and shocked by the coarseness of the strings and pulleys. In a similar way, psychology itself, when pushed to any nicety, discovers an abhorrent baldness, but rather from the fault of our analysis than from any poverty native to the mind. And perhaps in æsthetics the reason is the same: those disclosures which seem fatal to the dignity of art seem so perhaps only in the proportion of our ignorance; and those conscious and unconscious artifices which it seems unworthy of the serious artist to employ were yet, if we had the power to trace them to their springs, indications of a delicacy of the sense finer than we conceive, and hints of ancient harmonies in nature. This ignorance at least is largely irremediable. We shall never learn the affinities of beauty, for they lie too deep in nature and too far back in the mysterious history of man. The amateur, in consequence, will always grudgingly receive details of method, which can be stated but never can wholly be explained; nay, on the principle laid down in *Hudibras*, that

> 'Still the less they understand,
> The more they admire the sleight-of-hand,'

many are conscious at each new disclosure of a diminution in the ardour of their pleasure. I must therefore warn that well-known character, the general reader, that I am here embarked upon a most distasteful business: taking down the picture from the wall and looking on the back; and, like the inquiring child, pulling the musical cart to pieces.

1. *Choice of Words.*—The art of literature stands apart from among its sisters, because the material in which the literary artist works is the dialect of life; hence, on the one hand, a strange freshness and immediacy of address to the public mind, which is ready prepared to understand it; but hence, on the other, a singular limitation. The sister arts enjoy the use of a plastic and ductile material, like the modeller's clay; literature alone is condemned to work in mosaic with finite and quite rigid words. You have seen these blocks, dear to the nursery: this one a pillar, that a pediment, a third a window or a vase. It is with blocks of just such arbitrary size and figure that the literary architect is condemned to design the palace of his art. Nor is this all; for since these blocks, or words, are the acknowledged currency of our daily affairs, there are here possible none of those suppressions by which other arts obtain relief, continuity, and vigour: no hieroglyphic touch, no smoothed impasto, no inscrutable shadow, as in painting; no blank wall, as in architecture; but every word, phrase, sentence, and paragraph must move in a logical progression, and convey a definite conventional import.

Now the first merit which attracts in the pages of a good writer, or the talk of a brilliant conversationalist, is the apt choice and contrast of the words employed. It is, indeed, a strange art to take these blocks, rudely conceived for the purpose of the market or the bar, and by tact of application touch them to the finest meanings and distinctions, restore to them their primal energy, wittily shift them to another issue, or make of them a drum to rouse the passions. But though this form of merit is without doubt the most sensible and seizing, it is far from being equally present in all writers. The effect of words in Shakespeare, their singular justice, significance, and poetic charm, is different, indeed, from the effect of words in Addison or Fielding. Or, to take an example nearer home, the words in Carlyle seem electrified into an energy of lineament, like the faces of men furiously moved; whilst the words in Macaulay, apt enough to convey his meaning, harmonious enough in sound, yet glide from the memory like undistinguished elements in a general effect. But the first class of writers have no monopoly of literary merit. There is a sense in which Addison is superior to Carlyle; a sense in which Cicero is better than Tacitus, in which Voltaire excels Montaigne: it certainly lies not in the choice of words; it lies not in the interest or value of the matter; it lies not in force of intellect, of poetry, or of humour. The three first are but infants to the three second; and yet each, in a particular point of literary art, excels his superior in the whole.  What is that point?

2.  *The Web.*—Literature, although it stands apart by reason of the great destiny and general use of its medium in the affairs of men, is yet an art like other arts.  Of these we may distinguish two great classes: those arts, like sculpture, painting, acting, which are representative, or, as used to be said very clumsily, imitative; and those, like architecture, music, and the dance, which are self-sufficient, and merely presentative.  Each class, in right of this distinction, obeys principles apart; yet both may claim a common ground of existence, and it may be said with sufficient justice that the motive and end of any art whatever is to make a pattern; a pattern, it may be, of colours, of sounds, of changing attitudes, geometrical figures, or imitative lines; but still a pattern.  That is the plane on which these sisters meet; it is by this that they are arts; and if it be well they should at times forget their childish origin, addressing their intelligence to virile tasks, and performing unconsciously that necessary function of their life, to make a pattern, it is still imperative that the pattern shall be made.

Music and literature, the two temporal arts, contrive their pattern of sounds in time; or, in other words, of sounds and pauses.  Communication may be made in broken words, the business of life be carried on with substantives alone; but that is not what we call literature; and the true business of the literary artist is to plait or weave his meaning, involving it around itself; so that each sentence, by successive phrases, shall first come into a kind of knot, and then, after a moment of suspended meaning, solve and clear itself.  In every properly constructed sentence there should be observed this knot or hitch; so that (however delicately) we are led to foresee, to expect, and then to welcome the successive phrases.  The pleasure may be heightened by an element of surprise, as, very grossly, in the common figure of the antithesis, or, with much greater subtlety, where an antithesis is first suggested and then deftly evaded.  Each phrase, besides, is to be comely in itself; and between the implication and the evolution of the sentence there should be a satisfying equipoise of sound; for nothing more often disappoints the ear than a sentence solemnly and sonorously prepared, and hastily and weakly finished.  Nor should the balance be too striking and exact, for the one rule is to be infinitely various; to interest, to disappoint, to surprise, and yet still to gratify; to be ever changing, as it were, the stitch, and yet still to give the effect of an ingenious neatness.

The conjurer juggles with two oranges, and our pleasure in beholding him springs from this, that neither is for an instant overlooked or sacrificed. So with the writer. His pattern, which is to please the supersensual ear, is yet addressed, throughout and first of all, to the demands of logic. Whatever be the obscurities, whatever the intricacies of the argument, the neatness of the fabric must not suffer, or the artist has been proved unequal to his design. And, on the other hand, no form of words must be selected, no knot must be tied among the phrases, unless knot and word be precisely what is wanted to forward and illuminate the argument; for to fail in this is to swindle in the game. The genius of prose rejects the *cheville* no less emphatically than the laws of verse; and the *cheville*, I should perhaps explain to some of my readers, is any meaningless or very watered phrase employed to strike a balance in the sound. Pattern and argument live in each other; and it is by the brevity, clearness, charm, or emphasis of the second, that we judge the strength and fitness of the first.

Style is synthetic; and the artist, seeking, so to speak, a peg to plait about, takes up at once two or more elements or two or more views of the subject in hand; combines, implicates, and contrasts them; and while, in one sense, he was merely seeking an occasion for the necessary knot, he will be found, in the other, to have greatly enriched the meaning, or to have transacted the work of two sentences in the space of one. In the change from the successive shallow statements of the old chronicler to the dense and luminous flow of highly synthetic narrative, there is implied a vast amount of both philosophy and wit. The philosophy we clearly see, recognising in the synthetic writer a far more deep and stimulating view of life, and a far keener sense of the generation and affinity of events. The wit we might imagine to be lost; but it is not so, for it is just that wit, these perpetual nice contrivances, these difficulties overcome, this double purpose attained, these two oranges kept simultaneously dancing in the air, that, consciously or not, afford the reader his delight. Nay, and this wit, so little recognised, is the necessary organ of that philosophy which we so much admire. That style is therefore the most perfect, not, as fools say, which is the most natural, for the most natural is the disjointed babble of the chronicler; but which attains the highest degree of elegant and pregnant implication unobtrusively; or if obtrusively, then with the greatest gain to sense and vigour. Even the derangement of the phrases from their (so-called) natural order is luminous for the mind; and it is by the means of such designed reversal that the elements of a judgment may be most pertinently marshalled, or the stages of a complicated action most perspicuously bound into one.

The web, then, or the pattern: a web at once sensuous and logical, an elegant and pregnant texture: that is style, that is the foundation of the art of literature.  Books indeed continue to be read, for the interest of the fact or fable, in which this quality is poorly represented, but still it will be there.  And, on the other hand, how many do we continue to peruse and reperuse with pleasure whose only merit is the elegance of texture?  I am tempted to mention Cicero; and since Mr. Anthony Trollope is dead, I will.  It is a poor diet for the mind, a very colourless and toothless 'criticism of life'; but we enjoy the pleasure of a most intricate and dexterous pattern, every stitch a model at once of elegance and of good sense; and the two oranges, even if one of them be rotten, kept dancing with inimitable grace.

Up to this moment I have had my eye mainly upon prose; for though in verse also the implication of the logical texture is a crowning beauty, yet in verse it may be dispensed with.  You would think that here was a death-blow to all I have been saying; and far from that, it is but a new illustration of the principle involved.  For if the versifier is not bound to weave a pattern of his own, it is because another pattern has been formally imposed upon him by the laws of verse.  For that is the essence of a prosody.  Verse may be rhythmical; it may be merely alliterative; it may, like the French, depend wholly on the (quasi) regular recurrence of the rhyme; or, like the Hebrew, it may consist in the strangely fanciful device of repeating the same idea.  It does not matter on what principle the law is based, so it be a law.  It may be pure convention; it may have no inherent beauty; all that we have a right to ask of any prosody is, that it shall lay down a pattern for the writer, and that what it lays down shall be neither too easy nor too hard.  Hence it comes that it is much easier for men of equal facility to write fairly pleasing verse than reasonably interesting prose; for in prose the pattern itself has to be invented, and the difficulties first created before they can be solved.  Hence, again, there follows the peculiar greatness of the true versifier: such as Shakespeare, Milton, and Victor Hugo, whom I place beside them as versifier merely, not as poet.  These not only knit and knot the logical texture of the style with all the dexterity and strength of prose; they not only fill up the pattern of the verse with infinite variety and sober wit; but they give us, besides, a rare and special pleasure, by the art, comparable to that of counterpoint, with which they follow at the same time, and now contrast, and now combine, the double pattern of the texture and the verse.  Here the sounding line concludes; a little further on, the well-knit sentence; and yet a little further, and both will reach their solution on the same ringing syllable.  The best that can be offered by the best writer of prose is to show us the development of the idea and the stylistic pattern proceed hand in hand, sometimes by an obvious and triumphant effort, sometimes with a great air of ease and nature.  The writer of verse, by virtue of conquering another difficulty, delights us with a new series of triumphs.  He follows three purposes where his rival followed only two; and the change is of precisely the same nature as that from melody to harmony.  Or if you prefer to return to the juggler, behold him now, to the vastly increased enthusiasm of the spectators, juggling with three oranges instead of two.  Thus it is: added difficulty, added beauty; and the pattern, with every fresh element, becoming more interesting in itself.

Yet it must not be thought that verse is simply an addition; something is lost as well as something gained; and there remains plainly traceable, in comparing the best prose with the best verse, a certain broad distinction of method in the web.  Tight as the versifier may draw the knot of logic, yet for the ear he still leaves the tissue of the sentence floating somewhat loose.  In prose, the sentence turns upon a pivot, nicely balanced, and fits into itself with an obtrusive neatness like a puzzle.  The ear remarks and is singly gratified by this return and balance; while in verse it is all diverted to the measure.  To find comparable passages is hard; for either the versifier is hugely the superior of the rival, or, if he be not, and still persist in his more delicate enterprise, he fails to be as widely his inferior.  But let us select them from the pages of the same writer, one who was ambidexter; let us take, for instance, Rumour's Prologue to the Second Part of *Henry IV.*, a fine flourish of eloquence in Shakespeare's second manner, and set it side by side with Falstaff's praise of sherris, act iv. scene iii.; or let us compare the beautiful prose spoken throughout by Rosalind and Orlando; compare, for example, the first speech of all, Orlando's speech to Adam, with what passage it shall please you to select—the Seven Ages from the same play, or even such a stave of nobility as Othello's farewell to war; and still you will be able to perceive, if you have an ear for that class of music, a certain superior degree of organisation in the prose; a compacter fitting of the parts; a balance in the swing and the return as of a throbbing pendulum.  We must not, in things temporal, take from those who have little, the little that they have; the merits of prose are inferior, but they are not the same; it is a little kingdom, but an independent.

3.  *Rhythm of the Phrase.*—Some way back, I used a word which still awaits an application.  Each phrase, I said, was to be comely; but what is a comely phrase?  In all ideal and material points, literature, being a representative art, must look for analogies to painting and the like; but in what is technical and executive, being a temporal art, it must seek for them in music.  Each phrase of each sentence, like an air or a recitative in music, should be so artfully compounded out of long and short, out of accented and unaccented, as to gratify the sensual ear.  And of this the ear is the sole judge.  It is impossible to lay down laws.  Even in our accentual and rhythmic language no analysis can find the secret of the beauty of a verse; how much less, then, of those phrases, such as prose is built of, which obey no law but to be lawless and yet to please?  The little that we know of verse (and for my part I owe it all to my friend Professor Fleeming Jenkin) is, however, particularly interesting in the present connection.  We have been accustomed to describe the heroic line as five iambic feet, and to be filled with pain and confusion whenever, as by the conscientious schoolboy, we have heard our own description put in practice.

‘All night | the dreàd | less àn | gel ùn | pursùed,’

goes the schoolboy; but though we close our ears, we cling to our definition, in spite of its proved and naked insufficiency.  Mr. Jenkin was not so easily pleased, and readily discovered that the heroic line consists of four groups, or, if you prefer the phrase, contains four pauses:

‘All night | the dreadless | angel | unpursued.’

Four groups, each practically uttered as one word: the first, in this case, an iamb; the second, an amphibrachys; the third, a trochee; and the fourth, an amphimacer; and yet our schoolboy, with no other liberty but that of inflicting pain, had triumphantly scanned it as five iambs.  Perceive, now, this fresh richness of intricacy in the web; this fourth orange, hitherto unremarked, but still kept flying with the others.  What had seemed to be one thing it now appears is two; and, like some puzzle in arithmetic, the verse is made at the same time to read in fives and to read in fours.

But again, four is not necessary. We do not, indeed, find verses in six groups, because there is not room for six in the ten syllables; and we do not find verses of two, because one of the main distinctions of verse from prose resides in the comparative shortness of the group; but it is even common to find verses of three. Five is the one forbidden number; because five is the number of the feet; and if five were chosen, the two patterns would coincide, and that opposition which is the life of verse would instantly be lost. We have here a clue to the effect of polysyllables, above all in Latin, where they are so common and make so brave an architecture in the verse; for the polysyllable is a group of Nature's making. If but some Roman would return from Hades (Martial, for choice), and tell me by what conduct of the voice these thundering verses should be uttered—'*Aut Lacedæmonium Tarentum,*' for a case in point—I feel as if I should enter at last into the full enjoyment of the best of human verses.

But, again, the five feet are all iambic, or supposed to be; by the mere count of syllables the four groups cannot be all iambic; as a question of elegance, I doubt if any one of them requires to be so; and I am certain that for choice no two of them should scan the same. The singular beauty of the verse analysed above is due, so far as analysis can carry us, part, indeed, to the clever repetition of L, D, and N, but part to this variety of scansion in the groups. The groups which, like the bar in music, break up the verse for utterance, fall uniambically; and in declaiming a so-called iambic verse, it may so happen that we never utter one iambic foot. And yet to this neglect of the original beat there is a limit.

'Athens, the eye of Greece, mother of arts,'

is, with all its eccentricities, a good heroic line; for though it scarcely can be said to indicate the beat of the iamb, it certainly suggests no other measure to the ear. But begin

'Mother Athens, eye of Greece,'

or merely 'Mother Athens,' and the game is up, for the trochaic beat has been suggested. The eccentric scansion of the groups is an adornment; but as soon as the original beat has been forgotten, they cease implicitly to be eccentric. Variety is what is sought; but if we destroy the original mould, one of the terms of this variety is lost, and we fall back on sameness. Thus, both as to the arithmetical measure of the verse, and the degree of regularity in scansion, we see the laws of prosody to have one common purpose: to keep alive the opposition of two schemes simultaneously followed; to keep them notably apart, though still coincident; and to balance them with such judicial nicety before the reader, that neither shall be unperceived and neither signally prevail.

The rule of rhythm in prose is not so intricate. Here, too, we write in groups, or phrases, as I prefer to call them, for the prose phrase is greatly longer and is much more nonchalantly uttered than the group in verse; so that not only is there a greater interval of continuous sound between the pauses, but, for that very reason, word is linked more readily to word by a more summary enunciation. Still, the phrase is the strict analogue of the group, and successive phrases, like successive groups, must differ openly in length and rhythm. The rule of scansion in verse is to suggest no measure but the one in hand; in prose, to suggest no measure at all. Prose must be rhythmical, and it may be as much so as you will; but it must not be metrical. It may be anything, but it must not be verse. A single heroic line may very well pass and not disturb the somewhat larger stride of the prose style; but one following another will produce an instant impression of poverty, flatness, and disenchantment. The same lines delivered with the measured utterance of verse would perhaps seem rich in variety. By the more summary enunciation proper to prose, as to a more distant vision, these niceties of difference are lost. A whole verse is uttered as one phrase; and the ear is soon wearied by a succession of groups identical in length. The prose writer, in fact, since he is allowed to be so much less harmonious, is condemned to a perpetually fresh variety of movement on a larger scale, and must never disappoint the ear by the trot of an accepted metre. And this obligation is the third orange with which he has to juggle, the third quality which the prose writer must work into his pattern of words. It may be thought perhaps that this is a quality of ease rather than a fresh difficulty; but such is the inherently rhythmical strain of the English language, that the bad writer—and must I take for example that admired friend of my boyhood, Captain Reid?—the inexperienced writer, as Dickens in his earlier attempts to be impressive, and the jaded writer, as any one may see for himself, all tend to fall at once into the production of bad blank verse. And here it may be pertinently asked, Why bad? And I suppose it might be enough to answer that no man ever made good verse by accident, and that no verse can ever sound otherwise than trivial when uttered with the delivery of prose. But we can go beyond such answers. The weak side of verse is the regularity of the beat, which in itself is decidedly less impressive than the movement of the nobler prose; and it is just into this weak side, and this alone, that our careless writer falls. A peculiar density and mass, consequent on the nearness of the pauses, is one of the chief good qualities of verse; but this our accidental versifier, still following after the swift gait and large gestures of prose, does not so much as aspire to imitate. Lastly, since he remains unconscious that he is making verse at all, it can never occur to him to extract those effects of counterpoint and opposition which I have referred to as the final grace and justification of verse, and, I may add, of blank verse in particular.

4.  *Contents of the Phrase.*—Here is a great deal of talk about rhythm—and naturally; for in our canorous language rhythm is always at the door. But it must not be forgotten that in some languages this element is almost, if not quite, extinct, and that in our own it is probably decaying. The even speech of many educated Americans sounds the note of danger. I should see it go with something as bitter as despair, but I should not be desperate. As in verse no element, not even rhythm, is necessary, so, in prose also, other sorts of beauty will arise and take the place and play the part of those that we outlive. The beauty of the expected beat in verse, the beauty in prose of its larger and more lawless melody, patent as they are to English hearing, are already silent in the ears of our next neighbours; for in France the oratorical accent and the pattern of the web have almost or altogether succeeded to their places; and the French prose writer would be astounded at the labours of his brother across the Channel, and how a good quarter of his toil, above all *invita Minerva*, is to avoid writing verse. So wonderfully far apart have races wandered in spirit, and so hard it is to understand the literature next door!

Yet French prose is distinctly better than English; and French verse, above all while Hugo lives, it will not do to place upon one side. What is more to our purpose, a phrase or a verse in French is easily distinguishable as comely or uncomely. There is then another element of comeliness hitherto overlooked in this analysis: the contents of the phrase. Each phrase in literature is built of sounds, as each phrase in music consists of notes. One sound suggests, echoes, demands, and harmonises with another; and the art of rightly using these concordances is the final art in literature. It used to be a piece of good advice to all young writers to avoid alliteration; and the advice was sound, in so far as it prevented daubing. None the less for that, was it abominable nonsense, and the mere raving of those blindest of the blind who will not see. The beauty of the contents of a phrase, or of a sentence, depends implicitly upon alliteration and upon assonance. The vowel demands to be repeated; the consonant demands to be repeated; and both cry aloud to be perpetually varied. You may follow the adventures of a letter through any passage that has particularly pleased you; find it, perhaps, denied a while, to tantalise the ear; find it fired again at you in a whole broadside; or find it pass into congenerous sounds, one liquid or labial melting away into another. And you will find another and much stranger circumstance. Literature is written by and for two senses: a sort of internal ear, quick to perceive 'unheard melodies'; and the eye, which directs the pen and deciphers the printed phrase. Well, even as there are rhymes for the eye, so you will find that there are assonances and alliterations; that where an author is running the open A, deceived by the eye and our strange English spelling, he will often show a tenderness for the flat A; and that where he is running a particular consonant, he will not improbably rejoice to write it down even when it is mute or bears a different value.

Here, then, we have a fresh pattern—a pattern, to speak grossly, of letters—which makes the fourth preoccupation of the prose writer, and the fifth of the versifier. At times it is very delicate and hard to perceive, and then perhaps most excellent and winning (I say perhaps); but at times again the elements of this literal melody stand more boldly forward and usurp the ear. It becomes, therefore, somewhat a matter of conscience to select examples; and as I cannot very well ask the reader to help me, I shall do the next best by giving him the reason or the history of each selection. The two first, one in prose, one in verse, I chose without previous analysis, simply as engaging passages that had long re-echoed in my ear.

'I cannot praise a fugitive and cloistered virtue, unexercised and unbreathed, that never sallies out and sees her adversary, but slinks out of the race where that immortal garland is to be run for, not without dust and heat.' Down to 'virtue,' the current S and R are both announced and repeated unobtrusively, and by way of a grace-note that almost inseparable group PVF is given entire. The next phrase is a period of repose, almost ugly in itself, both S and R still audible, and B given as the last fulfilment of PVF. In the next four phrases, from 'that never' down to 'run for,' the mask is thrown off, and, but for a slight repetition of the F and V, the whole matter turns, almost too obtrusively, on S and R; first S coming to the front, and then R. In the concluding phrase all these favourite letters, and even the flat A, a timid preference for which is just perceptible, are discarded at a blow and in a bundle; and to make the break more obvious, every word ends with a dental, and all but one with T, for which we have been cautiously prepared since the beginning. The singular dignity of the first clause, and this hammer-stroke of the last, go far to make the charm of this exquisite sentence. But it is fair to own that S and R are used a little coarsely.

| 'In Xanady did Kubla Khan | (KĂNDL) |
|---|---|
| A stately pleasure dome decree, | (KDLSR) |
| Where Alph the sacred river ran, | (KĂNDLSR) |
| Through caverns measureless to man, | (KĂNLSR) |
| Down to a sunless sea.' | (NDLS) |

Here I have put the analysis of the main group alongside the lines; and the more it is looked at, the more interesting it will seem. But there are further niceties. In lines two and four, the current S is most delicately varied with Z. In line three, the current flat A is twice varied with the open A, already suggested in line two, and both times ('where' and 'sacred') in conjunction with the current R. In the same line F and V (a harmony in themselves, even when shorn of their comrade P) are admirably contrasted. And in line four there is a marked subsidiary M, which again was announced in line two. I stop from weariness, for more might yet be said.

My next example was recently quoted from Shakespeare as an example of the poet's colour sense. Now, I do not think literature has anything to do with colour, or poets anyway the better of such a sense; and I instantly attacked this passage, since 'purple' was the word that had so pleased the writer of the article, to see if there might not be some literary reason for its use. It will be seen that I succeeded amply; and I am bound to say I think the passage exceptional in Shakespeare— exceptional, indeed, in literature; but it was not I who chose it.

> 'The BaRge she sat iN, like a BURNished throNe
> BURNT oN the water: the POOP was BeateN gold,
> PURPle the sails and so PUR* Fumèd that    * per
> The wiNds were love-sick with them.'

It may be asked why I have put the F of 'perfumèd' in capitals; and I reply, because this change from P to F is the completion of that from B to P, already so adroitly carried out. Indeed, the whole passage is a monument of curious ingenuity; and it seems scarce worth while to indicate the subsidiary S, L, and W. In the same article, a second passage from Shakespeare was quoted, once again as an example of his colour sense:

> 'A mole cinque-spotted like the crimson drops
> I' the bottom of a cowslip.'

It is very curious, very artificial, and not worth while to analyse at length: I leave it to the reader. But before I turn my back on Shakespeare, I should like to quote a passage, for my own pleasure, and for a very model of every technical art:

> But in the wind and tempest of her frown,
>     W. P. V. F. (st) (ow)
> Distinction with a loud and powerful fan,
>     W. P. F. (st) (ow) L.
>
> Puffing at all, winnows the light away;
>     W. P. F. L.
> And what hath mass and matter by itself
>     W. F. L. M. A.
> Lies rich in virtue and unmingled.'
>     V. L. M.

From these delicate and choice writers I turned with some curiosity to a player of the big drum—Macaulay. I had in hand the two-volume edition, and I opened at the beginning of the second volume. Here was what I read:

'The violence of revolutions is generally proportioned to the degree of the maladministration which has produced them. It is therefore not strange that the government of Scotland, having been during many years greatly more corrupt than the government of England, should have fallen with a far heavier ruin. The movement against the last king of the house of Stuart was in England conservative, in Scotland destructive. The English complained not of the law, but of the violation of the law.'

This was plain-sailing enough; it was our old friend PVF, floated by the liquids in a body; but as I read on, and turned the page, and still found PVF with his attendant liquids, I confess my mind misgave me utterly. This could be no trick of Macaulay's; it must be the nature of the English tongue. In a kind of despair, I turned half-way through the volume; and coming upon his lordship dealing with General Cannon, and fresh from Claverhouse and Killiecrankie, here, with elucidative spelling, was my reward:

> 'Meanwhile the disorders of Kannon's Kamp went on inKreasing. He Kalled a Kouncil of war to Konsider what Kourse it would be advisable to taKe. But as soon as the Kouncil had met, a preliminary Kuestion was raised. The army was almost eKsKlusively a Highland army. The recent vKktory had been won eKsKlusively by Highland warriors. Great chie*f*s who had brought siKs or Se*v*en hundred *f*ighting men into the *f*ield did not think it *f*air that they should be out*v*oted by gentlemen *f*rom Ireland, and *f*rom the Low Kountries, who bore indeed King James's Kommission, and were Kalled Kolonels and Kaptains, but who were Kolonels without regiments and Kaptains without Kompanies.'

A moment of FV in all this world of K's! It was not the English language, then, that was an instrument of one string, but Macaulay that was an incomparable dauber.

It was probably from this barbaric love of repeating the same sound, rather than from any design of clearness, that he acquired his irritating habit of repeating words; I say the one rather than the other, because such a trick of the ear is deeper-seated and more original in man than any logical consideration. Few writers, indeed, are probably conscious of the length to which they push this melody of letters. One, writing very diligently, and only concerned about the meaning of his words and the rhythm of his phrases, was struck into amazement by the eager triumph with which he cancelled one expression to substitute another. Neither changed the sense; both being mono-syllables, neither could affect the scansion; and it was only by looking back on what he had already written that the mystery was solved: the second word contained an open A, and for nearly half a page he had been riding that vowel to the death.

In practice, I should add, the ear is not always so exacting; and ordinary writers, in ordinary moments, content themselves with avoiding what is harsh, and here and there, upon a rare occasion, buttressing a phrase, or linking two together, with a patch of assonance or a momentary jingle of alliteration.  To understand how constant is this preoccupation of good writers, even where its results are least obtrusive, it is only necessary to turn to the bad.  There, indeed, you will find cacophony supreme, the rattle of incongruous consonants only relieved by the jaw-breaking hiatus, and whole phrases not to be articulated by the powers of man.

*Conclusion.*—We may now briefly enumerate the elements of style. We have, peculiar to the prose writer, the task of keeping his phrases large, rhythmical, and pleasing to the ear, without ever allowing them to fall into the strictly metrical: peculiar to the versifier, the task of combining and contrasting his double, treble, and quadruple pattern, feet and groups, logic and metre—harmonious in diversity: common to both, the task of artfully combining the prime elements of language into phrases that shall be musical in the mouth; the task of weaving their argument into a texture of committed phrases and of rounded periods—but this particularly binding in the case of prose: and, again common to both, the task of choosing apt, explicit, and communicative words.  We begin to see now what an intricate affair is any perfect passage; how many faculties, whether of taste or pure reason, must be held upon the stretch to make it; and why, when it is made, it should afford us so complete a pleasure.  From the arrangement of according letters, which is altogether arabesque and sensual, up to the architecture of the elegant and pregnant sentence, which is a vigorous act of the pure intellect, there is scarce a faculty in man but has been exercised.  We need not wonder, then, if perfect sentences are rare, and perfect pages rarer.

# THE MORALITY OF THE PROFESSION OF LETTERS

The profession of letters has been lately debated in the public prints; and it has been debated, to put the matter mildly, from a point of view that was calculated to surprise high-minded men, and bring a general contempt on books and reading. Some time ago, in particular, a lively, pleasant, popular writer devoted an essay, lively and pleasant like himself, to a very encouraging view of the profession. We may be glad that his experience is so cheering, and we may hope that all others, who deserve it, shall be as handsomely rewarded; but I do not think we need be at all glad to have this question, so important to the public and ourselves, debated solely on the ground of money. The salary in any business under heaven is not the only, nor indeed the first, question. That you should continue to exist is a matter for your own consideration; but that your business should be first honest, and second useful, are points in which honour and morality are concerned. If the writer to whom I refer succeeds in persuading a number of young persons to adopt this way of life with an eye set singly on the livelihood, we must expect them in their works to follow profit only, and we must expect in consequence, if he will pardon me the epithets, a slovenly, base, untrue, and empty literature. Of that writer himself I am not speaking: he is diligent, clean, and pleasing; we all owe him periods of entertainment, and he has achieved an amiable popularity which he has adequately deserved. But the truth is, he does not, or did not when he first embraced it, regard his profession from this purely mercenary side. He went into it, I shall venture to say, if not with any noble design, at least in the ardour of a first love; and he enjoyed its practice long before he paused to calculate the wage. The other day an author was complimented on a piece of work, good in itself and exceptionally good for him, and replied, in terms unworthy of a commercial traveller that as the book was not briskly selling he did not give a copper farthing for its merit. It must not be supposed that the person to whom this answer was addressed received it as a profession of faith; he knew, on the other hand, that it was only a whiff of irritation; just as we know, when a respectable writer talks of literature as a way of life, like shoemaking, but not so useful, that he is only debating one aspect of a question, and is still clearly conscious of a dozen others more important in themselves and more central to the matter in hand.  But while those who treat literature in this penny-wise and virtue-foolish spirit are themselves truly in possession of a better light, it does not follow that the treatment is decent or improving, whether for themselves or others.  To treat all subjects in the highest, the most honourable, and the pluckiest spirit, consistent with the fact, is the first duty of a writer.  If he be well paid, as I am glad to hear he is, this duty becomes the more urgent, the neglect of it the more disgraceful. And perhaps there is no subject on which a man should speak so gravely as that industry, whatever it may be, which is the occupation or delight of his life; which is his tool to earn or serve with; and which, if it be unworthy, stamps himself as a mere incubus of dumb and greedy bowels on the shoulders of labouring humanity.  On that subject alone even to force the note might lean to virtue's side.  It is to be hoped that a numerous and enterprising generation of writers will follow and surpass the present one; but it would be better if the stream were stayed, and the roll of our old, honest English books were closed, than that esurient book-makers should continue and debase a brave tradition, and lower, in their own eyes, a famous race.  Better that our serene temples were deserted than filled with trafficking and juggling priests.

There are two just reasons for the choice of any way of life: the first is inbred taste in the chooser; the second some high utility in the industry selected.  Literature, like any other art, is singularly interesting to the artist; and, in a degree peculiar to itself among the arts, it is useful to mankind.  These are the sufficient justifications for any young man or woman who adopts it as the business of his life.  I shall not say much about the wages.  A writer can live by his writing. If not so luxuriously as by other trades, then less luxuriously.  The nature of the work he does all day will more affect his happiness than the quality of his dinner at night.  Whatever be your calling, and however much it brings you in the year, you could still, you know, get more by cheating.  We all suffer ourselves to be too much concerned about a little poverty; but such considerations should not move us in the choice of that which is to be the business and justification of so great a portion of our lives; and like the missionary, the patriot, or the philosopher, we should all choose that poor and brave career in which we can do the most and best for mankind. Now Nature, faithfully followed, proves herself a careful mother. A lad, for some liking to the jingle of words, betakes himself to letters for his life; by-and-by, when he learns more gravity, he finds that he has chosen better than he knew; that if he earns little, he is earning it amply; that if he receives a small wage, he is in a position to do considerable services; that it is in his power, in some small measure, to protect the oppressed and to defend the truth. So kindly is the world arranged, such great profit may arise from a small degree of human reliance on oneself, and such, in particular, is the happy star of this trade of writing, that it should combine pleasure and profit to both parties, and be at once agreeable, like fiddling, and useful, like good preaching.

This is to speak of literature at its highest; and with the four great elders who are still spared to our respect and admiration, with Carlyle, Ruskin, Browning, and Tennyson before us, it would be cowardly to consider it at first in any lesser aspect. But while we cannot follow these athletes, while we may none of us, perhaps, be very vigorous, very original, or very wise, I still contend that, in the humblest sort of literary work, we have it in our power either to do great harm or great good. We may seek merely to please; we may seek, having no higher gift, merely to gratify the idle nine days' curiosity of our contemporaries; or we may essay, however feebly, to instruct. In each of these we shall have to deal with that remarkable art of words which, because it is the dialect of life, comes home so easily and powerfully to the minds of men; and since that is so, we contribute, in each of these branches, to build up the sum of sentiments and appreciations which goes by the name of Public Opinion or Public Feeling. The total of a nation's reading, in these days of daily papers, greatly modifies the total of the nation's speech; and the speech and reading, taken together, form the efficient educational medium of youth. A good man or woman may keep a youth some little while in clearer air; but the contemporary atmosphere is all-powerful in the end on the average of mediocre characters. The copious Corinthian baseness of the American reporter or the Parisian *chroniquear*, both so lightly readable, must exercise an incalculable influence for ill; they touch upon all subjects, and on all with the same ungenerous hand; they begin the consideration of all, in young and unprepared minds, in an unworthy spirit; on all, they supply some pungency for dull people to quote. The mere body of this ugly matter overwhelms the rare utterances of good men; the sneering, the selfish, and the cowardly are scattered in broad sheets on every table, while the antidote, in small volumes, lies unread upon the shelf. I have spoken of the American and the French, not because they are so much baser, but so much more readable, than the English; their evil is done more effectively, in America for the masses, in French for the few that care to read; but with us as with them, the duties of literature are daily neglected, truth daily perverted and suppressed, and grave subjects daily degraded in the treatment. The journalist is not reckoned an important officer; yet judge of the good he might do, the harm he does; judge of it by one instance only: that when we find two journals on the reverse sides of politics each, on the same day, openly garbling a piece of news for the interest of its own party, we smile at the discovery (no discovery now!) as over a good joke and pardonable stratagem. Lying so open is scarce lying, it is true; but one of the things that we profess to teach our young is a respect for truth; and I cannot think this piece of education will be crowned with any great success, so long as some of us practise and the rest openly approve of public falsehood.

There are two duties incumbent upon any man who enters on the business of writing: truth to the fact and a good spirit in the treatment. In every department of literature, though so low as hardly to deserve the name, truth to the fact is of importance to the education and comfort of mankind, and so hard to preserve, that the faithful trying to do so will lend some dignity to the man who tries it. Our judgments are based upon two things: first, upon the original preferences of our soul; but, second, upon the mass of testimony to the nature of God, man, and the universe which reaches us, in divers manners, from without. For the most part these divers manners are reducible to one, all that we learn of past times and much that we learn of our own reaching us through the medium of books or papers, and even he who cannot read learning from the same source at second-hand and by the report of him who can. Thus the sum of the contemporary knowledge or ignorance of good and evil is, in large measure, the handiwork of those who write. Those who write have to see that each man's knowledge is, as near as they can make it, answerable to the facts of life; that he shall not suppose himself an angel or a monster; nor take this world for a hell; nor be suffered to imagine that all rights are concentred in his own caste or country, or all veracities in his own parochial creed.  Each man should learn what is within him, that he may strive to mend; he must be taught what is without him, that he may be kind to others.  It can never be wrong to tell him the truth; for, in his disputable state, weaving as he goes his theory of life, steering himself, cheering or reproving others, all facts are of the first importance to his conduct; and even if a fact shall discourage or corrupt him, it is still best that he should know it; for it is in this world as it is, and not in a world made easy by educational suppressions, that he must win his way to shame or glory.  In one word, it must always be foul to tell what is false; and it can never be safe to suppress what is true.  The very fact that you omit may be the fact which somebody was wanting, for one man's meat is another man's poison, and I have known a person who was cheered by the perusal of *Candide*.  Every fact is a part of that great puzzle we must set together; and none that comes directly in a writer's path but has some nice relations, unperceivable by him, to the totality and bearing of the subject under hand.  Yet there are certain classes of fact eternally more necessary than others, and it is with these that literature must first bestir itself.  They are not hard to distinguish, nature once more easily leading us; for the necessary, because the efficacious, facts are those which are most interesting to the natural mind of man.  Those which are coloured, picturesque, human, and rooted in morality, and those, on the other hand, which are clear, indisputable, and a part of science, are alone vital in importance, seizing by their interest, or useful to communicate.  So far as the writer merely narrates, he should principally tell of these.  He should tell of the kind and wholesome and beautiful elements of our life; he should tell unsparingly of the evil and sorrow of the present, to move us with instances: he should tell of wise and good people in the past, to excite us by example; and of these he should tell soberly and truthfully, not glossing faults, that we may neither grow discouraged with ourselves nor exacting to our neighbours.  So the body of contemporary literature, ephemeral and feeble in itself, touches in the minds of men the springs of thought and kindness, and supports them (for those who will go at all are easily supported) on their way to what is true and right.  And if, in any degree, it does so now, how much more might it do so if the writers chose!  There is not a life in all the records of the past but, properly studied, might lend a hint and a help to some contemporary.  There is not a juncture in to-day's affairs but some useful word may yet be said of it.  Even the reporter has an office, and, with clear eyes and honest language, may unveil injustices and point the way to progress. And for a last word: in all narration there is only one way to be clever, and that is to be exact. To be vivid is a secondary quality which must presuppose the first; for vividly to convey a wrong impression is only to make failure conspicuous.

But a fact may be viewed on many sides; it may be chronicled with rage, tears, laughter, indifference, or admiration, and by each of these the story will be transformed to something else. The newspapers that told of the return of our representatives from Berlin, even if they had not differed as to the facts, would have sufficiently differed by their spirits; so that the one description would have been a second ovation, and the other a prolonged insult. The subject makes but a trifling part of any piece of literature, and the view of the writer is itself a fact more important because less disputable than the others. Now this spirit in which a subject is regarded, important in all kinds of literary work, becomes all-important in works of fiction, meditation, or rhapsody; for there it not only colours but itself chooses the facts; not only modifies but shapes the work. And hence, over the far larger proportion of the field of literature, the health or disease of the writer's mind or momentary humour forms not only the leading feature of his work, but is, at bottom, the only thing he can communicate to others. In all works of art, widely speaking, it is first of all the author's attitude that is narrated, though in the attitude there be implied a whole experience and a theory of life. An author who has begged the question and reposes in some narrow faith cannot, if he would, express the whole or even many of the sides of this various existence; for, his own life being maim, some of them are not admitted in his theory, and were only dimly and unwillingly recognised in his experience. Hence the smallness, the triteness, and the inhumanity in works of merely sectarian religion; and hence we find equal although unsimilar limitation in works inspired by the spirit of the flesh or the despicable taste for high society. So that the first duty of any man who is to write is intellectual. Designedly or not, he has so far set himself up for a leader of the minds of men; and he must see that his own mind is kept supple, charitable, and bright. Everything but prejudice should find a voice through him; he should see the good in all things; where he has even a fear that he does not wholly understand, there he should be wholly silent; and he should recognise from the first that he has only one tool in his workshop, and that tool is sympathy.

The second duty, far harder to define, is moral. There are a thousand different humours in the mind, and about each of them, when it is uppermost, some literature tends to be deposited. Is this to be allowed? Not certainly in every case, and yet perhaps in more than rigourists would fancy. It were to be desired that all literary work, and chiefly works of art, issued from sound, human, healthy, and potent impulses, whether grave or laughing, humorous, romantic, or religious.

Yet it cannot be denied that some valuable books are partially insane; some, mostly religious, partially inhuman; and very many tainted with morbidity and impotence. We do not loathe a masterpiece although we gird against its blemishes. We are not, above all, to look for faults, but merits. There is no book perfect, even in design; but there are many that will delight, improve, or encourage the reader. On the one hand, the Hebrew psalms are the only religious poetry on earth; yet they contain sallies that savour rankly of the man of blood. On the other hand, Alfred de Musset had a poisoned and a contorted nature; I am only quoting that generous and frivolous giant, old Dumas, when I accuse him of a bad heart; yet, when the impulse under which he wrote was purely creative, he could give us works like *Carmosine* or *Fantasio*, in which the last note of the romantic comedy seems to have been found again to touch and please us. When Flaubert wrote *Madame Bovary*, I believe he thought chiefly of a somewhat morbid realism; and behold! the book turned in his hands into a masterpiece of appalling morality. But the truth is, when books are conceived under a great stress, with a soul of ninefold power, nine times heated and electrified by effort, the conditions of our being are seized with such an ample grasp, that, even should the main design be trivial or base, some truth and beauty cannot fail to be expressed. Out of the strong comes forth sweetness; but an ill thing poorly done is an ill thing top and bottom. And so this can be no encouragement to knock-kneed, feeble-wristed scribes, who must take their business conscientiously or be ashamed to practise it.

Man is imperfect; yet, in his literature, he must express himself and his own views and preferences; for to do anything else is to do a far more perilous thing than to risk being immoral: it is to be sure of being untrue.  To ape a sentiment, even a good one, is to travesty a sentiment; that will not be helpful.  To conceal a sentiment, if you are sure you hold it, is to take a liberty with truth.  There is probably no point of view possible to a sane man but contains some truth and, in the true connection, might be profitable to the race.  I am not afraid of the truth, if any one could tell it me, but I am afraid of parts of it impertinently uttered.  There is a time to dance and a time to mourn; to be harsh as well as to be sentimental; to be ascetic as well as to glorify the appetites; and if a man were to combine all these extremes into his work, each in its place and proportion, that work would be the world's masterpiece of morality as well as of art.  Partiality is immorality; for any book is wrong that gives a misleading picture of the world and life.  The trouble is that the weakling must be partial; the work of one proving dank and depressing; of another, cheap and vulgar; of a third, epileptically sensual; of a fourth, sourly ascetic.  In literature as in conduct, you can never hope to do exactly right.  All you can do is to make as sure as possible; and for that there is but one rule.  Nothing should be done in a hurry that can be done slowly.  It is no use to write a book and put it by for nine or even ninety years; for in the writing you will have partly convinced yourself; the delay must precede any beginning; and if you meditate a work of art, you should first long roll the subject under the tongue to make sure you like the flavour, before you brew a volume that shall taste of it from end to end; or if you propose to enter on the field of controversy, you should first have thought upon the question under all conditions, in health as well as in sickness, in sorrow as well as in joy.  It is this nearness of examination necessary for any true and kind writing, that makes the practice of the art a prolonged and noble education for the writer.

There is plenty to do, plenty to say, or to say over again, in the meantime.  Any literary work which conveys faithful facts or pleasing impressions is a service to the public.  It is even a service to be thankfully proud of having rendered.  The slightest novels are a blessing to those in distress, not chloroform itself a greater.  Our fine old sea-captain's life was justified when Carlyle soothed his mind with *The King's Own* or *Newton Forster*.  To please is to serve; and so far from its being difficult to instruct while you amuse, it is difficult to do the one thoroughly without the other.  Some part of the writer or his life will crop out in even a vapid book; and to read a novel that was conceived with any force is to multiply experience and to exercise the sympathies.

Every article, every piece of verse, every essay, every *entre-filet*, is destined to pass, however swiftly, through the minds of some portion of the public, and to colour, however transiently, their thoughts. When any subject falls to be discussed, some scribbler on a paper has the invaluable opportunity of beginning its discussion in a dignified and human spirit; and if there were enough who did so in our public press, neither the public nor the Parliament would find it in their minds to drop to meaner thoughts.  The writer has the chance to stumble, by the way, on something pleasing, something interesting, something encouraging, were it only to a single reader.  He will be unfortunate, indeed, if he suit no one.  He has the chance, besides, to stumble on something that a dull person shall be able to comprehend; and for a dull person to have read anything and, for that once, comprehended it, makes a marking epoch in his education.

Here, then, is work worth doing and worth trying to do well. And so, if I were minded to welcome any great accession to our trade, it should not be from any reason of a higher wage, but because it was a trade which was useful in a very great and in a very high degree; which every honest tradesman could make more serviceable to mankind in his single strength; which was difficult to do well and possible to do better every year; which called for scrupulous thought on the part of all who practised it, and hence became a perpetual education to their nobler natures; and which, pay it as you please, in the large majority of the best cases will still be underpaid.  For surely, at this time of day in the nineteenth century, there is nothing that an honest man should fear more timorously than getting and spending more than he deserves.

# BOOKS WHICH HAVE INFLUENCED ME

The Editor has somewhat insidiously laid a trap for his correspondents, the question put appearing at first so innocent, truly cutting so deep. It is not, indeed, until after some reconnaissance and review that the writer awakes to find himself engaged upon something in the nature of autobiography, or, perhaps worse, upon a chapter in the life of that little, beautiful brother whom we once all had, and whom we have all lost and mourned, the man we ought to have been, the man we hoped to be. But when word has been passed (even to an editor), it should, if possible, be kept; and if sometimes I am wise and say too little, and sometimes weak and say too much, the blame must lie at the door of the person who entrapped me.

The most influential books, and the truest in their influence, are works of fiction. They do not pin the reader to a dogma, which he must afterwards discover to be inexact; they do not teach him a lesson, which he must afterwards unlearn. They repeat, they rearrange, they clarify the lessons of life; they disengage us from ourselves, they constrain us to the acquaintance of others; and they show us the web of experience, not as we can see it for ourselves, but with a singular change—that monstrous, consuming *ego* of ours being, for the nonce, struck out. To be so, they must be reasonably true to the human comedy; and any work that is so serves the turn of instruction. But the course of our education is answered best by those poems and romances where we breathe a magnanimous atmosphere of thought and meet generous and pious characters. Shakespeare has served me best. Few living friends have had upon me an influence so strong for good as Hamlet or Rosalind. The last character, already well beloved in the reading, I had the good fortune to see, I must think, in an impressionable hour, played by Mrs. Scott Siddons. Nothing has ever more moved, more delighted, more refreshed me; nor has the influence quite passed away. Kent's brief speech over the dying

Lear had a great effect upon my mind, and was the burthen of my reflections for long, so profoundly, so touchingly generous did it appear in sense, so overpowering in expression. Perhaps my dearest and best friend outside of Shakespeare is D'Artagnan—the elderly D'Artagnan of the *Vicomte de Bragelonne.* I know not a more human soul, nor, in his way, a finer; I shall be very sorry for the man who is so much of a pedant in morals that he cannot learn from the Captain of Musketeers. Lastly, I must name the *Pilgrim's Progress*, a book that breathes of every beautiful and valuable emotion.

But of works of art little can be said; their influence is profound and silent, like the influence of nature; they mould by contact; we drink them up like water, and are bettered, yet know not how. It is in books more specifically didactic that we can follow out the effect, and distinguish and weigh and compare. A book which has been very influential upon me fell early into my hands, and so may stand first, though I think its influence was only sensible later on, and perhaps still keeps growing, for it is a book not easily outlived: the *Essais* of Montaigne. That temperate and genial picture of life is a great gift to place in the hands of persons of to-day; they will find in these smiling pages a magazine of heroism and wisdom, all of an antique strain; they will have their 'linen decencies' and excited orthodoxies fluttered, and will (if they have any gift of reading) perceive that these have not been fluttered without some excuse and ground of reason; and (again if they have any gift of reading) they will end by seeing that this old gentleman was in a dozen ways a finer fellow, and held in a dozen ways a nobler view of life, than they or their contemporaries.

The next book, in order of time, to influence me, was the New Testament, and in particular the Gospel according to St. Matthew. I believe it would startle and move any one if they could make a certain effort of imagination and read it freshly like a book, not droningly and dully like a portion of the Bible. Any one would then be able to see in it those truths which we are all courteously supposed to know and all modestly refrain from applying. But upon this subject it is perhaps better to be silent.

I come next to Whitman's *Leaves of Grass*, a book of singular service, a book which tumbled the world upside down for me, blew into space a thousand cobwebs of genteel and ethical illusion, and, having thus shaken my tabernacle of lies, set me back again upon a strong foundation of all the original and manly virtues. But it is, once more, only a book for those who have the gift of reading. I will be very frank—I believe it is so with all good books except, perhaps, fiction. The average man lives, and must live, so wholly in convention, that gunpowder charges of the truth are more apt to discompose than to invigorate his creed. Either he cries out upon blasphemy and indecency, and crouches the closer round that little idol of part-truths and part-conveniences which is the contemporary deity, or he is convinced by what is new, forgets what is old, and becomes truly blasphemous and indecent himself. New truth is only useful to supplement the old; rough truth is only wanted to expand, not to destroy, our civil and often elegant conventions. He who cannot judge had better stick to fiction and the daily papers. There he will get little harm, and, in the first at least, some good.

Close upon the back of my discovery of Whitman, I came under the influence of Herbert Spencer. No more persuasive rabbi exists, and few better. How much of his vast structure will bear the touch of time, how much is clay and how much brass, it were too curious to inquire. But his words, if dry, are always manly and honest; there dwells in his pages a spirit of highly abstract joy, plucked naked like an algebraic symbol but still joyful; and the reader will find there a *caput mortuum* of piety, with little indeed of its loveliness, but with most of its essentials; and these two qualities make him a wholesome, as his intellectual vigour makes him a bracing, writer. I should be much of a hound if I lost my gratitude to Herbert Spencer.

*Goethe's Life*, by Lewes, had a great importance for me when it first fell into my hands—a strange instance of the partiality of man's good and man's evil. I know no one whom I less admire than Goethe; he seems a very epitome of the sins of genius, breaking open the doors of private life, and wantonly wounding friends, in that crowning offence of *Werther*, and in his own character a mere pen-and-ink Napoleon, conscious of the rights and duties of superior talents as a Spanish inquisitor was conscious of the rights and duties of his office. And yet in his fine devotion to his art, in his honest and serviceable friendship for Schiller, what lessons are contained! Biography, usually so false to its office, does here for once perform for us some of the work of fiction, reminding us, that is, of the truly mingled tissue of man's nature, and how huge faults and shining virtues cohabit and persevere in the same character. History serves us well to this effect, but in the originals, not in the pages of the popular epitomiser, who is bound, by the very nature of his task, to make us feel the difference of epochs instead of the essential identity of man, and even in the originals only to those who can recognise their own human virtues and defects in strange forms, often inverted and under strange names, often interchanged. Martial is a poet of no good repute, and it gives a man new thoughts to read his works dispassionately, and find in this unseemly jester's serious passages the image of a kind, wise, and self-respecting gentleman. It is customary, I suppose, in reading Martial, to leave out these pleasant verses; I never heard of them, at least, until I found them for myself; and this partiality is one among a thousand things that help to build up our distorted and hysterical conception of the great Roman Empire.

This brings us by a natural transition to a very noble book—the *Meditations* of Marcus Aurelius. The dispassionate gravity, the noble forgetfulness of self, the tenderness of others, that are there expressed and were practised on so great a scale in the life of its writer, make this book a book quite by itself. No one can read it and not be moved. Yet it scarcely or rarely appeals to the feelings—those very mobile, those not very trusty parts of man. Its address lies further back: its lesson comes more deeply home; when you have read, you carry away with you a memory of the man himself; it is as though you had touched a loyal hand, looked into brave eyes, and made a noble friend; there is another bond on you thenceforward, binding you to life and to the love of virtue.

Wordsworth should perhaps come next. Every one has been influenced by Wordsworth, and it is hard to tell precisely how. A certain innocence, a rugged austerity of joy, a sight of the stars, 'the silence that is in the lonely hills,' something of the cold thrill of dawn, cling to his work and give it a particular address to what is best in us. I do not know that you learn a lesson; you need not—Mill did not—agree with any one of his beliefs; and yet the spell is cast. Such are the best teachers; a dogma learned is only a new error—the old one was perhaps as good; but a spirit communicated is a perpetual possession. These best teachers climb beyond teaching to the plane of art; it is themselves, and what is best in themselves, that they communicate.

I should never forgive myself if I forgot *The Egoist*. It is art, if you like, but it belongs purely to didactic art, and from all the novels I have read (and I have read thousands) stands in a place by itself.

Here is a Nathan for the modern David; here is a book to send the blood into men's faces.  Satire, the angry picture of human faults, is not great art; we can all be angry with our neighbour; what we want is to be shown, not his defects, of which we are too conscious, but his merits, to which we are too blind.  And *The Egoist* is a satire; so much must be allowed; but it is a satire of a singular quality, which tells you nothing of that obvious mote, which is engaged from first to last with that invisible beam.  It is yourself that is hunted down; these are your own faults that are dragged into the day and numbered, with lingering relish, with cruel cunning and precision.  A young friend of Mr. Meredith's (as I have the story) came to him in an agony.  'This is too bad of you,' he cried.  'Willoughby is me!'  'No, my dear fellow,' said the author; 'he is all of us.'

I have read *The Egoist* five or six times myself, and I mean to read it again; for I am like the young friend of the anecdote—I think Willoughby an unmanly but a very serviceable exposure of myself.

I suppose, when I am done, I shall find that I have forgotten much that was most influential, as I see already I have forgotten Thoreau, and Hazlitt, whose paper 'On the Spirit of Obligations' was a turning-point in my life, and Penn, whose little book of aphorisms had a brief but strong effect on me, and Mitford's *Tales of Old Japan*, wherein I learned for the first time the proper attitude of any rational man to his country's laws—a secret found, and kept, in the Asiatic islands.  That I should commemorate all is more than I can hope or the Editor could ask.  It will be more to the point, after having said so much upon improving books, to say a word or two about the improvable reader.  The gift of reading, as I have called it, is not very common, nor very generally understood.  It consists, first of all, in a vast intellectual endowment—a free grace, I find I must call it—by which a man rises to understand that he is not punctually right, nor those from whom he differs absolutely wrong. He may hold dogmas; he may hold them passionately; and he may know that others hold them but coldly, or hold them differently, or hold them not at all. Well, if he has the gift of reading, these others will be full of meat for him.  They will see the other side of propositions and the other side of virtues.  He need not change his dogma for that, but he may change his reading of that dogma, and he must supplement and correct his deductions from it.  A human truth, which is always very much a lie, hides as much of life as it displays.  It is men who hold another truth, or, as it seems to us, perhaps, a dangerous lie, who can extend our restricted field of knowledge, and rouse our drowsy consciences. Something that seems quite new, or that seems insolently false or very dangerous, is the test of a reader. If he tries to see what it means, what truth excuses it, he has the gift, and let him read. If he is merely hurt, or offended, or exclaims upon his author's folly, he had better take to the daily papers; he will never be a reader.

And here, with the aptest illustrative force, after I have laid down my part-truth, I must step in with its opposite. For, after all, we are vessels of a very limited content. Not all men can read all books; it is only in a chosen few that any man will find his appointed food; and the fittest lessons are the most palatable, and make themselves welcome to the mind. A writer learns this early, and it is his chief support; he goes on unafraid, laying down the law; and he is sure at heart that most of what he says is demonstrably false, and much of a mingled strain, and some hurtful, and very little good for service; but he is sure besides that when his words fall into the hands of any genuine reader, they will be weighed and winnowed, and only that which suits will be assimilated; and when they fall into the hands of one who cannot intelligently read, they come there quite silent and inarticulate, falling upon deaf ears, and his secret is kept as if he had not written.

# A NOTE ON REALISM

Style is the invariable mark of any master; and for the student who does not aspire so high as to be numbered with the giants, it is still the one quality in which he may improve himself at will. Passion, wisdom, creative force, the power of mystery or colour, are allotted in the hour of birth, and can be neither learned nor simulated. But the just and dexterous use of what qualities we have, the proportion of one part to another and to the whole, the elision of the useless, the accentuation of the important, and the preservation of a uniform character from end to end—these, which taken together constitute technical perfection, are to some degree within the reach of industry and intellectual courage. What to put in and what to leave out; whether some particular fact be organically necessary or purely ornamental; whether, if it be purely ornamental, it may not weaken or obscure the general design; and finally, whether, if we decide to use it, we should do so grossly and notably, or in some conventional disguise: are questions of plastic style continually rearising. And the sphinx that patrols the highways of executive art has no more unanswerable riddle to propound.

In literature (from which I must draw my instances) the great change of the past century has been effected by the admission of detail. It was inaugurated by the romantic Scott; and at length, by the semi-romantic Balzac and his more or less wholly unromantic followers, bound like a duty on the novelist. For some time it signified and expressed a more ample contemplation of the conditions of man's life; but it has recently (at least in France) fallen into a merely technical and decorative stage, which it is, perhaps, still too harsh to call survival. With a movement of alarm, the wiser or more timid begin to fall a little back from these extremities; they begin to aspire after a more naked, narrative articulation; after the succinct, the dignified, and the poetic; and as a means to this, after a general lightening of this baggage of detail. After Scott we beheld the starveling story—

once, in the hands of Voltaire, as abstract as a parable—begin to be pampered upon facts. The introduction of these details developed a particular ability of hand; and that ability, childishly indulged, has led to the works that now amaze us on a railway journey. A man of the unquestionable force of M. Zola spends himself on technical successes. To afford a popular flavour and attract the mob, he adds a steady current of what I may be allowed to call the rancid. That is exciting to the moralist; but what more particularly interests the artist is this tendency of the extreme of detail, when followed as a principle, to degenerate into mere *feux-de-joie* of literary tricking. The other day even M. Daudet was to be heard babbling of audible colours and visible sounds.

This odd suicide of one branch of the realists may serve to remind us of the fact which underlies a very dusty conflict of the critics. All representative art, which can be said to live, is both realistic and ideal; and the realism about which we quarrel is a matter purely of externals. It is no especial cultus of nature and veracity, but a mere whim of veering fashion, that has made us turn our back upon the larger, more various, and more romantic art of yore. A photographic exactitude in dialogue is now the exclusive fashion; but even in the ablest hands it tells us no more—I think it even tells us less—than Molière, wielding his artificial medium, has told to us and to all time of Alceste or Orgon, Dorine or Chrysale. The historical novel is forgotten. Yet truth to the conditions of man's nature and the conditions of man's life, the truth of literary art, is free of the ages. It may be told us in a carpet comedy, in a novel of adventure, or a fairy tale. The scene may be pitched in London, on the sea-coast of Bohemia, or away on the mountains of Beulah. And by an odd and luminous accident, if there is any page of literature calculated to awake the envy of M. Zola, it must be that *Troilus and Cressida* which Shakespeare, in a spasm of unmanly anger with the world, grafted on the heroic story of the siege of Troy.

This question of realism, let it then be clearly understood, regards not in the least degree the fundamental truth, but only the technical method, of a work of art. Be as ideal or as abstract as you please, you will be none the less veracious; but if you be weak, you run the risk of being tedious and inexpressive; and if you be very strong and honest, you may chance upon a masterpiece.

A work of art is first cloudily conceived in the mind; during the period of gestation it stands more clearly forward from these swaddling mists, puts on expressive lineaments, and becomes at length that most faultless, but also, alas! that incommunicable product of the human mind, a perfected design. On the approach to execution all is changed. The artist must now step down, don his working clothes, and become the artisan. He now resolutely commits his airy conception, his delicate Ariel, to the touch of matter; he must decide, almost in a breath, the scale, the style, the spirit, and the particularity of execution of his whole design.

The engendering idea of some works is stylistic; a technical preoccupation stands them instead of some robuster principle of life. And with these the execution is but play; for the stylistic problem is resolved beforehand, and all large originality of treatment wilfully foregone. Such are the verses, intricately designed, which we have learnt to admire, with a certain smiling admiration, at the hands of Mr. Lang and Mr. Dobson; such, too, are those canvases where dexterity or even breadth of plastic style takes the place of pictorial nobility of design. So, it may be remarked, it was easier to begin to write *Esmond* than *Vanity Fair*, since, in the first, the style was dictated by the nature of the plan; and Thackeray, a man probably of some indolence of mind, enjoyed and got good profit of this economy of effort. But the case is exceptional. Usually in all works of art that have been conceived from within outwards, and generously nourished from the author's mind, the moment in which he begins to execute is one of extreme perplexity and strain. Artists of indifferent energy and an imperfect devotion to their own ideal make this ungrateful effort once for all; and, having formed a style, adhere to it through life. But those of a higher order cannot rest content with a process which, as they continue to employ it, must infallibly degenerate towards the academic and the cut-and-dried. Every fresh work in which they embark is the signal for a fresh engagement of the whole forces of their mind; and the changing views which accompany the growth of their experience are marked by still more sweeping alterations in the manner of their art. So that criticism loves to dwell upon and distinguish the varying periods of a Raphael, a Shakespeare, or a Beethoven.

It is, then, first of all, at this initial and decisive moment when execution is begun, and thenceforth only in a less degree, that the ideal and the real do indeed, like good and evil angels, contend for the direction of the work. Marble, paint, and language, the pen, the needle, and the brush, all have their grossnesses, their ineffable impotences, their hours, if I may so express myself, of insubordination. It is the work and it is a great part of the delight of any artist to contend with these unruly tools, and now by brute energy, now by witty expedient, to drive and coax them to effect his will. Given these means, so laughably inadequate, and given the interest, the intensity, and the multiplicity of the actual sensation whose effect he is to render with their aid, the artist has one main and necessary resource which he must, in every case and upon any theory, employ. He must, that is, suppress much and omit more. He must omit what is tedious or irrelevant, and suppress what is tedious and necessary. But such facts as, in regard to the main design, subserve a variety of purposes, he will perforce and eagerly retain. And it is the mark of the very highest order of creative art to be woven exclusively of such. There, any fact that is registered is contrived a double or a treble debt to pay, and is at once an ornament in its place, and a pillar in the main design. Nothing would find room in such a picture that did not serve, at once, to complete the composition, to accentuate the scheme of colour, to distinguish the planes of distance, and to strike the note of the selected sentiment; nothing would be allowed in such a story that did not, at the same time, expedite the progress of the fable, build up the characters, and strike home the moral or the philosophical design. But this is unattainable. As a rule, so far from building the fabric of our works exclusively with these, we are thrown into a rapture if we think we can muster a dozen or a score of them, to be the plums of our confection. And hence, in order that the canvas may be filled or the story proceed from point to point, other details must be admitted. They must be admitted, alas! upon a doubtful title; many without marriage robes. Thus any work of art, as it proceeds towards completion, too often—I had almost written always—loses in force and poignancy of main design. Our little air is swamped and dwarfed among hardly relevant orchestration; our little passionate story drowns in a deep sea of descriptive eloquence or slipshod talk.

But again, we are rather more tempted to admit those particulars which we know we can describe; and hence those most of all which, having been described very often, have grown to be conventionally treated in the practice of our art. These we choose, as the mason chooses the acanthus to adorn his capital, because they come naturally to the accustomed hand. The old stock incidents and accessories, tricks of workmanship and schemes of composition (all being admirably good, or they would long have been forgotten) haunt and tempt our fancy, offer us ready-made but not perfectly appropriate solutions for any problem that arises, and wean us from the study of nature and the uncompromising practice of art. To struggle, to face nature, to find fresh solutions, and give expression to facts which have not yet been adequately or not yet elegantly expressed, is to run a little upon the danger of extreme self-love. Difficulty sets a high price upon achievement; and the artist may easily fall into the error of the French naturalists, and consider any fact as welcome to admission if it be the ground of brilliant handiwork; or, again, into the error of the modern landscape-painter, who is apt to think that difficulty overcome and science well displayed can take the place of what is, after all, the one excuse and breath of art—charm. A little further, and he will regard charm in the light of an unworthy sacrifice to prettiness, and the omission of a tedious passage as an infidelity to art.

We have now the matter of this difference before us. The idealist, his eye singly fixed upon the greater outlines, loves rather to fill up the interval with detail of the conventional order, briefly touched, soberly suppressed in tone, courting neglect. But the realist, with a fine intemperance, will not suffer the presence of anything so dead as a convention; he shall have all fiery, all hot-pressed from nature, all charactered and notable, seizing the eye. The style that befits either of these extremes, once chosen, brings with it its necessary disabilities and dangers. The immediate danger of the realist is to sacrifice the beauty and significance of the whole to local dexterity, or, in the insane pursuit of completion, to immolate his readers under facts; but he comes in the last resort, and as his energy declines, to discard all design, abjure all choice, and, with scientific thoroughness, steadily to communicate matter which is not worth learning. The danger of the idealist is, of course, to become merely null and lose all grip of fact, particularity, or passion.

We talk of bad and good. Everything, indeed, is good which is conceived with honesty and executed with communicative ardour. But though on neither side is dogmatism fitting, and though in every case the artist must decide for himself, and decide afresh and yet afresh for each succeeding work and new creation; yet one thing may be generally said, that we of the last quarter of the nineteenth century, breathing as we do the intellectual atmosphere of our age, are more apt to err upon the side of realism than to sin in quest of the ideal.  Upon that theory it may be well to watch and correct our own decisions, always holding back the hand from the least appearance of irrelevant dexterity, and resolutely fixed to begin no work that is not philosophical, passionate, dignified, happily mirthful, or, at the last and least, romantic in design.

# MY FIRST BOOK:
# 'TREASURE ISLAND'

It was far indeed from being my first book, for I am not a novelist alone. But I am well aware that my paymaster, the Great Public, regards what else I have written with indifference, if not aversion; if it call upon me at all, it calls on me in the familiar and indelible character; and when I am asked to talk of my first book, no question in the world but what is meant is my first novel.

Sooner or later, somehow, anyhow, I was bound to write a novel. It seems vain to ask why. Men are born with various manias: from my earliest childhood, it was mine to make a plaything of imaginary series of events; and as soon as I was able to write, I became a good friend to the paper-makers. Reams upon reams must have gone to the making of 'Rathillet,' 'The Pentland Rising,' 'The King's Pardon' (otherwise 'Park Whitehead'), 'Edward Daven,' 'A Country Dance,' and 'A Vendetta in the West'; and it is consolatory to remember that these reams are now all ashes, and have been received again into the soil. I have named but a few of my ill-fated efforts, only such indeed as came to a fair bulk ere they were desisted from; and even so they cover a long vista of years. 'Rathillet' was attempted before fifteen, 'The Vendetta' at twenty-nine, and the succession of defeats lasted unbroken till I was thirty-one. By that time, I had written little books and little essays and short stories; and had got patted on the back and paid for them—though not enough to live upon. I had quite a reputation, I was the successful man; I passed my days in toil, the futility of which would sometimes make my cheek to burn—that I should spend a man's energy upon this business, and yet could not earn a livelihood: and still there shone ahead of me an unattained ideal: although I had attempted the thing with vigour not less than ten or twelve times, I had not yet written a novel. All—all my pretty ones—had gone for a little, and then stopped inexorably like a schoolboy's watch. I might be compared to a cricketer of many years' standing who should never have made a run.  Anybody can write a short story—a bad one, I mean—who has industry and paper and time enough; but not every one may hope to write even a bad novel.  It is the length that kills.

The accepted novelist may take his novel up and put it down, spend days upon it in vain, and write not any more than he makes haste to blot.  Not so the beginner.  Human nature has certain rights; instinct—the instinct of self-preservation—forbids that any man (cheered and supported by the consciousness of no previous victory) should endure the miseries of unsuccessful literary toil beyond a period to be measured in weeks.  There must be something for hope to feed upon.  The beginner must have a slant of wind, a lucky vein must be running, he must be in one of those hours when the words come and the phrases balance of themselves—*even to begin*.  And having begun, what a dread looking forward is that until the book shall be accomplished!  For so long a time, the slant is to continue unchanged, the vein to keep running, for so long a time you must keep at command the same quality of style: for so long a time your puppets are to be always vital, always consistent, always vigorous! I remember I used to look, in those days, upon every three-volume novel with a sort of veneration, as a feat—not possibly of literature— but at least of physical and moral endurance and the courage of Ajax.

In the fated year I came to live with my father and mother at Kinnaird, above Pitlochry.  Then I walked on the red moors and by the side of the golden burn; the rude, pure air of our mountains inspirited, if it did not inspire us, and my wife and I projected a joint volume of logic stories, for which she wrote 'The Shadow on the Bed,' and I turned out 'Thrawn Janet,' and a first draft of 'The Merry Men.'  I love my native air, but it does not love me; and the end of this delightful period was a cold, a fly-blister, and a migration by Strathairdle and Glenshee to the Castleton of Braemar.

There it blew a good deal and rained in a proportion; my native air was more unkind than man's ingratitude, and I must consent to pass a good deal of my time between four walls in a house lugubriously known as the Late Miss McGregor's Cottage.  And now admire the finger of predestination.  There was a schoolboy in the Late Miss McGregor's Cottage, home from the holidays, and much in want of 'something craggy to break his mind upon.'  He had no thought of literature; it was the art of Raphael that received his fleeting suffrages;

and with the aid of pen and ink and a shilling box of water colours, he had soon turned one of the rooms into a picture gallery. My more immediate duty towards the gallery was to be showman; but I would sometimes unbend a little, join the artist (so to speak) at the easel, and pass the afternoon with him in a generous emulation, making coloured drawings. On one of these occasions, I made the map of an island; it was elaborately and (I thought) beautifully coloured; the shape of it took my fancy beyond expression; it contained harbours that pleased me like sonnets; and with the unconsciousness of the predestined, I ticketed my performance 'Treasure Island.' I am told there are people who do not care for maps, and find it hard to believe. The names, the shapes of the woodlands, the courses of the roads and rivers, the prehistoric footsteps of man still distinctly traceable up hill and down dale, the mills and the ruins, the ponds and the ferries, perhaps the *Standing Stone* or the *Druidic Circle* on the heath; here is an inexhaustible fund of interest for any man with eyes to see or twopence-worth of imagination to understand with! No child but must remember laying his head in the grass, staring into the infinitesimal forest and seeing it grow populous with fairy armies.

Somewhat in this way, as I paused upon my map of 'Treasure Island,' the future character of the book began to appear there visibly among imaginary woods; and their brown faces and bright weapons peeped out upon me from unexpected quarters, as they passed to and fro, fighting and hunting treasure, on these few square inches of a flat projection. The next thing I knew I had some papers before me and was writing out a list of chapters. How often have I done so, and the thing gone no further! But there seemed elements of success about this enterprise. It was to be a story for boys; no need of psychology or fine writing; and I had a boy at hand to be a touchstone. Women were excluded. I was unable to handle a brig (which the *Hispaniola* should have been), but I thought I could make shift to sail her as a schooner without public shame. And then I had an idea for John Silver from which I promised myself funds of entertainment; to take an admired friend of mine (whom the reader very likely knows and admires as much as I do), to deprive him of all his finer qualities and higher graces of temperament, to leave him with nothing but his strength, his courage, his quickness, and his magnificent geniality, and to try to express these in terms of the culture of a raw tarpaulin. Such psychical surgery is, I think, a common way of 'making character'; perhaps it is, indeed, the only way. We can put in the quaint figure that spoke a hundred words with us yesterday by the wayside; but do we know him?  Our friend, with his infinite variety and flexibility, we know—but can we put him in?  Upon the first, we must engraft secondary and imaginary qualities, possibly all wrong; from the second, knife in hand, we must cut away and deduct the needless arborescence of his nature, but the trunk and the few branches that remain we may at least be fairly sure of.

On a chill September morning, by the cheek of a brisk fire, and the rain drumming on the window, I began *The Sea Cook*, for that was the original title.  I have begun (and finished) a number of other books, but I cannot remember to have sat down to one of them with more complacency.  It is not to be wondered at, for stolen waters are proverbially sweet.  I am now upon a painful chapter.  No doubt the parrot once belonged to Robinson Crusoe.  No doubt the skeleton is conveyed from Poe.  I think little of these, they are trifles and details; and no man can hope to have a monopoly of skeletons or make a corner in talking birds.  The stockade, I am told, is from *Masterman Ready*.  It may be, I care not a jot.  These useful writers had fulfilled the poet's saying: departing, they had left behind them Footprints on the sands of time, Footprints which perhaps another—and I was the other!  It is my debt to Washington Irving that exercises my conscience, and justly so, for I believe plagiarism was rarely carried farther.  I chanced to pick up the *Tales of a Traveller* some years ago with a view to an anthology of prose narrative, and the book flew up and struck me: Billy Bones, his chest, the company in the parlour, the whole inner spirit, and a good deal of the material detail of my first chapters—all were there, all were the property of Washington Irving.  But I had no guess of it then as I sat writing by the fireside, in what seemed the spring-tides of a somewhat pedestrian inspiration; nor yet day by day, after lunch, as I read aloud my morning's work to the family.  It seemed to me original as sin; it seemed to belong to me like my right eye.  I had counted on one boy, I found I had two in my audience.  My father caught fire at once with all the romance and childishness of his original nature.  His own stories, that every night of his life he put himself to sleep with, dealt perpetually with ships, roadside inns, robbers, old sailors, and commercial travellers before the era of steam.  He never finished one of these romances; the lucky man did not require to!  But in *Treasure Island* he recognised something kindred to his own imagination; it was *his* kind of picturesque; and he not only heard with delight the daily chapter, but set himself acting to collaborate. When the time came for Billy Bones's chest to be ransacked, he must have passed the better part of a day preparing, on the back of a legal envelope, an inventory of its contents, which I exactly followed; and the name of 'Flint's old ship'—the *Walrus*—was given at his particular request. And now who should come dropping in, *ex machinâ*, but Dr. Japp, like the disguised prince who is to bring down the curtain upon peace and happiness in the last act; for he carried in his pocket, not a horn or a talisman, but a publisher—had, in fact, been charged by my old friend, Mr. Henderson, to unearth new writers for *Young Folks*. Even the ruthlessness of a united family recoiled before the extreme measure of inflicting on our guest the mutilated members of *The Sea Cook*; at the same time, we would by no means stop our readings; and accordingly the tale was begun again at the beginning, and solemnly re-delivered for the benefit of Dr. Japp. From that moment on, I have thought highly of his critical faculty; for when he left us, he carried away the manuscript in his portmanteau.

Here, then, was everything to keep me up, sympathy, help, and now a positive engagement. I had chosen besides a very easy style. Compare it with the almost contemporary 'Merry Men', one reader may prefer the one style, one the other—'tis an affair of character, perhaps of mood; but no expert can fail to see that the one is much more difficult, and the other much easier to maintain. It seems as though a full-grown experienced man of letters might engage to turn out *Treasure Island* at so many pages a day, and keep his pipe alight. But alas! this was not my case. Fifteen days I stuck to it, and turned out fifteen chapters; and then, in the early paragraphs of the sixteenth, ignominiously lost hold. My mouth was empty; there was not one word of *Treasure Island* in my bosom; and here were the proofs of the beginning already waiting me at the 'Hand and Spear'! Then I corrected them, living for the most part alone, walking on the heath at Weybridge in dewy autumn mornings, a good deal pleased with what I had done, and more appalled than I can depict to you in words at what remained for me to do. I was thirty-one; I was the head of a family; I had lost my health; I had never yet paid my way, never yet made £200 a year; my father had quite recently bought back and cancelled a book that was judged a failure: was this to be another and last fiasco? I was indeed very close on despair; but I shut my mouth hard, and during the journey to Davos, where I was to pass the winter, had the resolution to think of other things and bury myself in the novels of M. de Boisgobey. Arrived at my destination, down I sat one morning to the unfinished tale; and behold! it flowed from me like small talk; and in a second tide of delighted industry, and again at a rate of a chapter a day, I finished *Treasure Island*. It had to be transcribed almost exactly; my wife was ill; the schoolboy remained alone of the faithful; and John Addington Symonds (to whom I timidly mentioned what I was engaged on) looked on me askance. He was at that time very eager I should write on the characters of Theophrastus: so far out may be the judgments of the wisest men. But Symonds (to be sure) was scarce the confidant to go to for sympathy on a boy's story. He was large-minded; 'a full man,' if there was one; but the very name of my enterprise would suggest to him only capitulations of sincerity and solecisms of style. Well! he was not far wrong.

*Treasure Island*—it was Mr. Henderson who deleted the first title, *The Sea Cook*—appeared duly in the story paper, where it figured in the ignoble midst, without woodcuts, and attracted not the least attention. I did not care. I liked the tale myself, for much the same reason as my father liked the beginning: it was my kind of picturesque. I was not a little proud of John Silver, also; and to this day rather admire that smooth and formidable adventurer. What was infinitely more exhilarating, I had passed a landmark; I had finished a tale, and written 'The End' upon my manuscript, as I had not done since 'The Pentland Rising,' when I was a boy of sixteen not yet at college. In truth it was so by a set of lucky accidents; had not Dr. Japp come on his visit, had not the tale flowed from me with singular case, it must have been laid aside like its predecessors, and found a circuitous and unlamented way to the fire. Purists may suggest it would have been better so. I am not of that mind. The tale seems to have given much pleasure, and it brought (or, was the means of bringing) fire and food and wine to a deserving family in which I took an interest. I need scarcely say I mean my own.

But the adventures of *Treasure Island* are not yet quite at an end. I had written it up to the map. The map was the chief part of my plot. For instance, I had called an islet 'Skeleton Island,' not knowing what I meant, seeking only for the immediate picturesque, and it was to justify this name that I broke into the gallery of Mr. Poe and stole Flint's pointer. And in the same way, it was because I had made two harbours that the *Hispaniola* was sent on her wanderings with Israel

Hands.  The time came when it was decided to republish, and I sent in my manuscript, and the map along with it, to Messrs. Cassell.  The proofs came, they were corrected, but I heard nothing of the map.  I wrote and asked; was told it had never been received, and sat aghast. It is one thing to draw a map at random, set a scale in one corner of it at a venture, and write up a story to the measurements.  It is quite another to have to examine a whole book, make an inventory of all the allusions contained in it, and with a pair of compasses, painfully design a map to suit the data.  I did it; and the map was drawn again in my father's office, with embellishments of blowing whales and sailing ships, and my father himself brought into service a knack he had of various writing, and elaborately *forged* the signature of Captain Flint, and the sailing directions of Billy Bones.  But somehow it was never *Treasure Island* to me.

I have said the map was the most of the plot.  I might almost say it was the whole.  A few reminiscences of Poe, Defoe, and Washington Irving, a copy of Johnson's *Buccaneers*, the name of the Dead Man's Chest from Kingsley's *At Last*, some recollections of canoeing on the high seas, and the map itself, with its infinite, eloquent suggestion, made up the whole of my materials.  It is, perhaps, not often that a map figures so largely in a tale, yet it is always important.  The author must know his countryside, whether real or imaginary, like his hand; the distances, the points of the compass, the place of the sun's rising, the behaviour of the moon, should all be beyond cavil. And how troublesome the moon is!  I have come to grief over the moon in *Prince Otto*, and so soon as that was pointed out to me, adopted a precaution which I recommend to other men—I never write now without an almanack.  With an almanack, and the map of the country, and the plan of every house, either actually plotted on paper or already and immediately apprehended in the mind, a man may hope to avoid some of the grossest possible blunders.  With the map before him, he will scarce allow the sun to set in the east, as it does in *The Antiquary*.  With the almanack at hand, he will scarce allow two horsemen, journeying on the most urgent affair, to employ six days, from three of the Monday morning till late in the Saturday night, upon a journey of, say, ninety or a hundred miles, and before the week is out, and still on the same nags, to cover fifty in one day, as may be read at length in the inimitable novel of *Rob Roy*.  And it is certainly well, though far from necessary, to avoid such 'croppers.'  But it is my contention—my superstition, if you like—that who is faithful to his map, and consults it, and draws from it his inspiration, daily and hourly, gains positive support, and not mere negative immunity from accident.  The tale has a root there; it grows in that soil; it has a spine of its own behind the words.  Better if the country be real, and he has walked every foot of it and knows every milestone.  But even with imaginary places, he will do well in the beginning to provide a map; as he studies it, relations will appear that he had not thought upon; he will discover obvious, though unsuspected, short-cuts and footprints for his messengers; and even when a map is not all the plot, as it was in *Treasure Island*, it will be found to be a mine of suggestion.

# THE GENESIS OF 'THE MASTER OF BALLANTRAE'

I was walking one night in the verandah of a small house in which I lived, outside the hamlet of Saranac. It was winter; the night was very dark; the air extraordinary clear and cold, and sweet with the purity of forests. From a good way below, the river was to be heard contending with ice and boulders: a few lights appeared, scattered unevenly among the darkness, but so far away as not to lessen the sense of isolation. For the making of a story here were fine conditions. I was besides moved with the spirit of emulation, for I had just finished my third or fourth perusal of *The Phantom Ship*. 'Come,' said I to my engine, 'let us make a tale, a story of many years and countries, of the sea and the land, savagery and civilisation; a story that shall have the same large features, and may be treated in the same summary elliptic method as the book you have been reading and admiring.' I was here brought up with a reflection exceedingly just in itself, but which, as the sequel shows, I failed to profit by. I saw that Marryat, not less than Homer, Milton, and Virgil, profited by the choice of a familiar and legendary subject; so that he prepared his readers on the very title-page; and this set me cudgelling my brains, if by any chance I could hit upon some similar belief to be the centre-piece of my own meditated fiction. In the course of this vain search there cropped up in my memory a singular case of a buried and resuscitated fakir, which I had been often told by an uncle of mine, then lately dead, Inspector-General John Balfour.

On such a fine frosty night, with no wind and the thermometer below zero, the brain works with much vivacity; and the next moment I had seen the circumstance transplanted from India and the tropics to the Adirondack wilderness and the stringent cold of the Canadian border. Here then, almost before I had begun my story, I had two countries, two of the ends of the earth involved: and thus though the notion of the resuscitated man failed entirely on the score of general acceptation, or even (as I have since found) acceptability, it fitted at once with my design of a tale of many lands; and this decided me to consider further of its possibilities. The man who should thus be buried was the first question: a good man, whose return to life would be hailed by the reader and the other characters with gladness? This trenched upon the Christian picture, and was dismissed. If the idea, then, was to be of any use at all for me, I had to create a kind of evil genius to his friends and family, take him through many disappearances, and make this final restoration from the pit of death, in the icy American wilderness, the last and the grimmest of the series. I need not tell my brothers of the craft that I was now in the most interesting moment of an author's life; the hours that followed that night upon the balcony, and the following nights and days, whether walking abroad or lying wakeful in my bed, were hours of unadulterated joy. My mother, who was then living with me alone, perhaps had less enjoyment; for, in the absence of my wife, who is my usual helper in these times of parturition, I must spur her up at all seasons to hear me relate and try to clarify my unformed fancies.

And while I was groping for the fable and the character required, behold I found them lying ready and nine years old in my memory. Pease porridge hot, pease porridge cold, pease porridge in the pot, nine years old. Was there ever a more complete justification of the rule of Horace? Here, thinking of quite other things, I had stumbled on the solution, or perhaps I should rather say (in stagewright phrase) the Curtain or final Tableau of a story conceived long before on the moors between Pitlochry and Strathardle, conceived in Highland rain, in the blend of the smell of heather and bog-plants, and with a mind full of the Athole correspondence and the memories of the dumlicide Justice. So long ago, so far away it was, that I had first evoked the faces and the mutual tragic situation of the men of Durrisdeer.

My story was now world-wide enough: Scotland, India, and America being all obligatory scenes. But of these India was strange to me except in books; I had never known any living Indian save a Parsee, a member of my club in London, equally civilised, and (to all seeing) equally accidental with myself. It was plain, thus far, that I should have to get into India and out of it again upon a foot of fairy lightness; and I believe this first suggested to me the idea of the Chevalier Burke for a narrator. It was at first intended that he should be Scottish, and I was then filled with fears that he might prove only the degraded shadow of my own Alan Breck.  Presently, however, it began to occur to me it would be like my Master to curry favour with the Prince's Irishmen; and that an Irish refugee would have a particular reason to find himself in India with his countryman, the unfortunate Lally.  Irish, therefore, I decided he should be, and then, all of a sudden, I was aware of a tall shadow across my path, the shadow of Barry Lyndon.  No man (in Lord Foppington's phrase) of a nice morality could go very deep with my Master: in the original idea of this story conceived in Scotland, this companion had been besides intended to be worse than the bad elder son with whom (as it was then meant) he was to visit Scotland; if I took an Irishman, and a very bad Irishman, in the midst of the eighteenth century, how was I to evade Barry Lyndon?  The wretch besieged me, offering his services; he gave me excellent references; he proved that he was highly fitted for the work I had to do; he, or my own evil heart, suggested it was easy to disguise his ancient livery wit a little lace and a few frogs and buttons, so that Thackeray himself should hardly recognise him.  And then of a sudden there came to me memories of a young Irishman, with whom I was once intimate, and had spent long nights walking and talking with, upon a very desolate coast in a bleak autumn: I recalled him as a youth of an extraordinary moral simplicity—almost vacancy; plastic to any influence, the creature of his admirations: and putting such a youth in fancy into the career of a soldier of fortune, it occurred to me that he would serve my turn as well as Mr. Lyndon, and in place of entering into competition with the Master, would afford a slight though a distinct relief.  I know not if I have done him well, though his moral dissertations always highly entertained me: but I own I have been surprised to find that he reminded some critics of Barry Lyndon after all. . . .

# PREFACE TO 'THE MASTER OF BALLANTRAE'

Although an old, consistent exile, the editor of the following pages revisits now and again the city of which he exults to be a native; and there are few things more strange, more painful, or more salutary, than such revisitations. Outside, in foreign spots, he comes by surprise and awakens more attention than he had expected; in his own city, the relation is reversed, and he stands amazed to be so little recollected. Elsewhere he is refreshed to see attractive faces, to remark possible friends; there he scouts the long streets, with a pang at heart, for the faces and friends that are no more. Elsewhere he is delighted with the presence of what is new, there tormented by the absence of what is old. Elsewhere he is content to be his present self; there he is smitten with an equal regret for what he once was and for what he once hoped to be.

He was feeling all this dimly, as he drove from the station, on his last visit; he was feeling it still as he alighted at the door of his friend Mr. Johnstone Thomson, W.S., with whom he was to stay. A hearty welcome, a face not altogether changed, a few words that sounded of old days, a laugh provoked and shared, a glimpse in passing of the snowy cloth and bright decanters and the Piranesis on the dining-room wall, brought him to his bed-room with a somewhat lightened cheer, and when he and Mr. Thomson sat down a few minutes later, cheek by jowl, and pledged the past in a preliminary bumper, he was already almost consoled, he had already almost forgiven himself his two unpardonable errors, that he should ever have left his native city, or ever returned to it.

'I have something quite in your way,' said Mr. Thomson. 'I wished to do honour to your arrival; because, my dear fellow, it is my own youth that comes back along with you; in a very tattered and withered state, to be sure, but—well!—all that's left of it.'

'A great deal better than nothing,' said the editor. 'But what is this which is quite in my way?'

'I was coming to that,' said Mr. Thomson: 'Fate has put it in my power to honour your arrival with something really original by way of dessert. A mystery.'

'A mystery?' I repeated.

'Yes,' said his friend, 'a mystery. It may prove to be nothing, and it may prove to be a great deal. But in the meanwhile it is truly mysterious, no eye having looked on it for near a hundred years; it is highly genteel, for it treats of a titled family; and it ought to be melodramatic, for (according to the superscription) it is concerned with death.'

'I think I rarely heard a more obscure or a more promising annunciation,' the other remarked. 'But what is It?'

'You remember my predecessor's, old Peter M'Brair's business?'

'I remember him acutely; he could not look at me without a pang of reprobation, and he could not feel the pang without betraying it. He was to me a man of a great historical interest, but the interest was not returned.'

'Ah well, we go beyond him,' said Mr. Thomson. 'I daresay old Peter knew as little about this as I do. You see, I succeeded to a prodigious accumulation of old law-papers and old tin boxes, some of them of Peter's hoarding, some of his father's, John, first of the dynasty, a great man in his day. Among other collections were all the papers of the Durrisdeers.'

'The Durrisdeers!' cried I. 'My dear fellow, these may be of the greatest interest. One of them was out in the '45; one had some strange passages with the devil—you will find a note of it in Law's*Memorials*, I think; and there was an unexplained tragedy, I know not what, much later, about a hundred years ago—'

'More than a hundred years ago,' said Mr. Thomson. 'In 1783.'

'How do you know that? I mean some death.'

'Yes, the lamentable deaths of my lord Durrisdeer and his brother, the Master of Ballantrae (attainted in the troubles),' said Mr. Thomson with something the tone of a man quoting. 'Is that it?'

'To say truth,' said I, 'I have only seen some dim reference to the things in memoirs; and heard some traditions dimmer still, through my uncle (whom I think you knew). My uncle lived when he was a boy in the neighbourhood of St. Bride's; he has often told me of the avenue closed up and grown over with grass, the great gates never opened, the last lord and his old maid sister who lived in the back parts of the house, a quiet, plain, poor, hum-drum couple it would seem—but pathetic too, as the last of that stirring and brave house—and, to the country folk, faintly terrible from some deformed traditions.'

'Yes,' said Mr. Thomson. Henry Graeme Durie, the last lord, died in 1820; his sister, the Honourable Miss Katherine Durie, in '27; so much I know; and by what I have been going over the last few days, they were what you say, decent, quiet people and not rich. To say truth, it was a letter of my lord's that put me on the search for the packet we are going to open this evening. Some papers could not be found; and he wrote to Jack M'Brair suggesting they might be among those sealed up by a Mr. Mackellar. M'Brair answered, that the papers in question were all in Mackellar's own hand, all (as the writer understood) of a purely narrative character; and besides, said he, "I am bound not to open them before the year 1889." You may fancy if these words struck me: I instituted a hunt through all the M'Brair repositories; and at last hit upon that packet which (if you have had enough wine) I propose to show you at once.'

In the smoking-room, to which my host now led me, was a packet, fastened with many seals and enclosed in a single sheet of strong paper thus endorsed:—

Papers relating to the lives and lamentable deaths of the late Lord Durisdeer, and his elder brother James, commonly called Master of Ballantrae, attainted in the troubles: entrusted into the hands of John M'Brair in the Lawnmarket of Edinburgh, W.S.; this 20th day of September Anno Domini 1789; by him to be kept secret until the revolution of one hundred years complete, or until the 20th day of September 1889: the same compiled and written by me,

EPHRAIM MACKELLAR,
*For near forty years Land Steward on the*
*estates of His Lordship.*

As Mr. Thomson is a married man, I will not say what hour had struck when we laid down the last of the following pages; but I will give a few words of what ensued.

'Here,' said Mr. Thomson, 'is a novel ready to your hand: all you have to do is to work up the scenery, develop the characters, and improve the style.'

'My dear fellow,' said I, 'they are just the three things that I would rather die than set my hand to.  It shall be published as it stands.'

'But it's so bald,' objected Mr. Thomson.

'I believe there is nothing so noble as baldness,' replied I, 'and I am sure there is nothing so interesting.  I would have all literature bald, and all authors (if you like) but one.'

'Well, well,' said Mr. Thomson, 'we shall see.'

Made in the USA
Monee, IL
07 July 2026